CHESTER A. ARTHUR

ENCYCLOPEDIA
of PRESIDENTS

Chester A. Arthur

Twenty-First President of the United States

By Charnan Simon

Consultant: Charles Abele, Ph.D.
Social Studies Instructor
Chicago Public School System

 CHILDRENS PRESS®

CHICAGO

Arthur takes the presidential oath upon Garfield's death.

Library of Congress Cataloging-in-Publication Data

Simon, Charnan.
    Chester A. Arthur / By Charnan Simon.
      p.   cm. — (Encyclopedia of presidents)
    Includes index.
    Summary: Traces the life of the young lawyer who rose up
through New York's political machine to become the twenty-
first president of the United States.
    ISBN 0-516-01369-6
    1. Arthur, Chester Alan, 1829-1886—Juvenile literature.
2. Presidents—United States—Biography—Juvenile
literature. I. Title. II. Series
E692.S56   1989   89-35386
973.8'4'092—dc20   CIP
[B]   AC

Picture Acknowledgments

AP/Wide World Photos, Inc.—30, 36, 37, 42
(bottom), 48, 52, 57, 65 (bottom), 84, 87

The Bettmann Archive—4, 5, 9, 13 (2 photos),
17, 20, 22 (top), 27, 32 (top), 38, 39, 45, 46, 56,
58, 59, 60, 61, 64 (2 photos), 65 (top), 72 (top),
76, 77, 81, 82, 83 (bottom), 88

Historical Pictures Service, Chicago—6, 8 (2
photos), 10, 14, 19, 22 (bottom), 28, 32
(bottom), 34, 44 (2 photos), 47, 50, 53, 54, 62,
66, 69, 72 (bottom), 73 (2 photos), 78 (2 photos),
79 (2 photos), 80, 89

North Wind Picture Archives—18, 23 (2
photos), 24, 26, 33, 40, 42 (top), 51, 67, 83 (top)

U.S. Bureau of Printing and Engraving—2

Cover design and illustration
by Steven Gaston Dobson

President Arthur welcomes
President-elect Grover Cleveland
to the White House before Arthur
leaves office in 1885.

Table of Contents

Chapter 1

A Somber Summer

The summer of 1881 was a somber one for citizens of the United States. On July 2, an assassin's bullet had seriously wounded President James A. Garfield as he walked through the Washington, D.C., railroad depot.

For weeks Garfield fought for his life in the steamy Washington summer. Though doctors probed and prodded, they could not locate the bullet they knew had lodged somewhere near his spine. In the end, their attentions only made the president's condition worse, as their unclean instruments increased the infection already spreading through his weakened body. Fearing the worst, Garfield's family finally took the invalid to their summer home in Elberon, New Jersey, where they hoped the fresh sea breezes might revive him.

While the president languished on his sickbed, the country as a whole languished, too. Without an able president at the helm, government ground to a virtual halt. Congress went into recess, there were no cabinet meetings, there was no executive action. There was, in fact, no executive. With the president disabled, no one seemed to know who was in charge.

Opposite page: President Garfield's
ambulance train on the way to Elberon

7

Above: President Garfield is wounded in a Washington train depot.
Below: Doctors try to locate the bullet in Garfield's body.

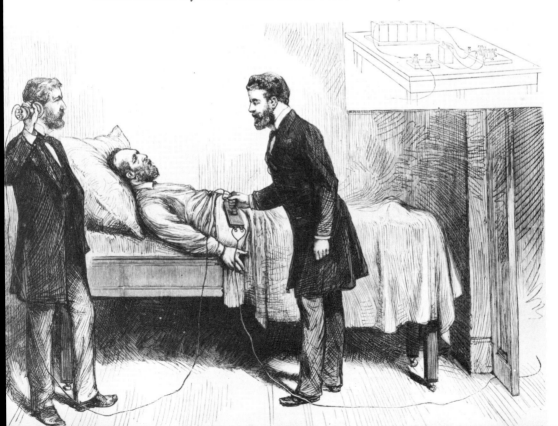

GREAT REVIVAL OF "HARMONY"

Arthur is shown trying to make peace between political rivals.

The U.S. Constitution was of little help here. In case of the president's "inability to discharge" his duties, the Constitution says that "the same shall devolve on the Vice-President." But who was to say that the president was unable to perform his duties? Congress? The president himself? The vice-president?

It was this last possibility that kept the nation uneasy during that long, hot summer of 1881. Vice-President Chester A. Arthur was nobody's idea of the ideal chief executive. First of all, Arthur was a confirmed product of the "spoils system" of New York's political machine. He had made his mark in the New York State political arena and was known to be a puppet of the powerful senator from that state, Roscoe Conkling. Though Arthur himself was not suspected of being corrupt, he made no secret of his allegiance to Conkling's Stalwart faction of the Republican Party. Who knew what he would do as president?

The powerful senator Roscoe Conkling

Then, too, Arthur had never before held any sort of elected office. In fact he had been nominated to the vice-presidency simply to appease the powerful Conkling, whose Stalwart candidate for president was passed over at the 1880 Republican convention.

There was still another cause for concern about Chester A. Arthur. He had first been appointed to public office in 1871, as collector of customs (import and export taxes) for the Port of New York. The New York Custom House was notorious for being staffed with men who got their jobs as a reward for loyal party activity — and who kept their jobs by doing little or nothing except fattening their own wallets. Again, though Arthur himself did not profit by his stint at the custom house, he had largely ignored the corruption going on around him. In 1877, President Rutherford B. Hayes had suspended him from the position.

All in all, Chester Arthur's reputation was not a shining one. It didn't help that Garfield's assassin, a disgruntled office-seeker named Charles J. Guiteau, had announced when arrested, "I did it and will go to jail for it. I am a Stalwart, and Arthur will be President." Though no one seriously believed that Arthur (or the Stalwarts) had anything to do with Garfield's shooting, it was not a good omen for the man who stood next in line to be president of the United States.

Former president Hayes seemed to sum up the nation's feelings when he wrote in his diary: "The death of the President at this time would be a national calamity whose consequences we can not now confidently conjecture. Arthur for President! Conkling the power behind the throne, superior to the throne!"

And what was Chester Arthur's own opinion of the tragic sequence of events that threatened to propel him to the presidency? When approached by a reporter after Garfield's shooting, he asked, "What can I say? What is there to be said by me? I am overwhelmed with grief over the awful news." When another reporter mentioned Guiteau's boast of being a Stalwart, Arthur reacted angrily. "No one," he said, "deplores the calamity more than Senator Conkling and myself. . . . All personal considerations and political views must be merged in the national sorrow. I am an American among millions of Americans grieving for their wounded chief." When the first medical reports of Garfield's condition suggested that the president might recover, Arthur responded, "As the President gets better I get better, too."

Since these first medical reports were so positive, Arthur soon left Washington, D.C., for his New York City home. He had never wanted to be president, and he refused to take any action that might make it look as if he were eager to assume the office. Throughout the summer, his anxiety over his wounded chief was as great as the nation's.

Finally, on September 19, the newsboys in the street began crying, "Garfield dying! The President is dying!" The dreaded news was confirmed in a telegram Arthur received from the cabinet warning that Garfield's end was near. By 11:30 that evening the news was final—Garfield was dead.

Reporters rushed to Arthur's New York home to get a statement from him. They were turned away, however, by doorkeeper Alec Powell. "I daren't ask him," Powell said. "He is sitting alone in his room sobbing like a child, with his head on his desk and his face buried in his hands. I dare not disturb him."

What much of the nation had dreaded had now happened. Chester A. Arthur was the twenty-first president of the United States. As one horrified citizen exclaimed, "Chet Arthur, President of the United States? Good God!"

But would the worst really come to pass? Would Arthur prove to be just a pawn in Roscoe Conkling's hands? Or would Governor Foster of Ohio instead prove correct in his prediction that "The people and the politicians will find that Vice-President Arthur and President Arthur are different men."

Only time would tell.

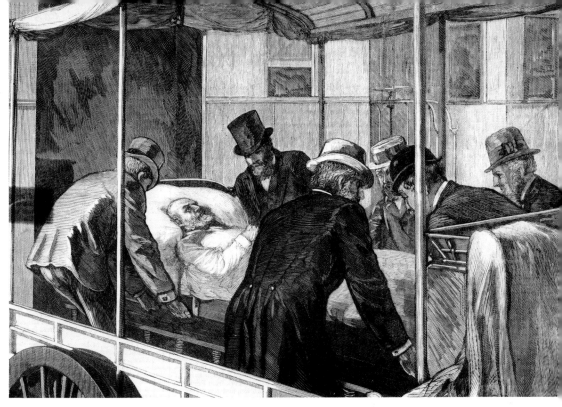

Above: Garfield is moved to an ambulance train car.
Below: President Garfield on his deathbed in 1881

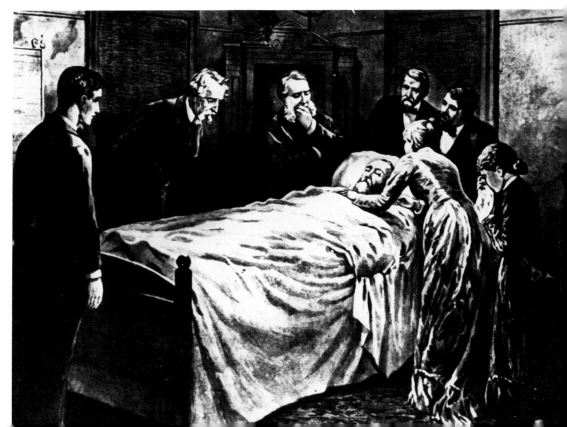

The log cabin where Chester Arthur was born in Fairfield, Vermont

Chapter 2

Elder Arthur's Boy

It is said that when Chester Alan Arthur was born, his father danced with joy. "Elder" William Arthur was a feisty Scotch-Irishman who had abandoned his early ambitions as a teacher and lawyer to become a Baptist preacher. He was ordained in May 1828, and within a month had moved his Vermont-born wife, Malvina, and their four daughters to the site of his first parish in Fairfield, Vermont.

Fairfield was not a prosperous town. While the congregation struggled to build a parsonage for their new minister and his expanding family, the six Arthurs lived in a tiny log cabin. It was in this crude cabin that Malvina gave birth, on October 5, 1829, to her fifth child—and first son. One shocked parishioner recalled disapprovingly, "When I announced the boy to Elder Arthur he danced up and down the room."

Elder Arthur was frequently given to shocking his flock. He was a passionate, often sarcastic preacher. And as his parishioners soon learned, he did not suffer fools (or sinners!) in silence. He also held staunch abolitionist beliefs—not a popular stand in the 1830s, thirty years before the question of slavery would tear the Union apart in the Civil War. Understandably, he had frequent quarrels with parishioners, deacons, and trustees.

Elder Arthur's boundless energy, barbed tongue, and unpopular opinions caused the family to change parishes often. Young Chester moved five times during his first nine years, before the family finally settled in Union Village (now Greenwich), New York, in late 1839.

The Arthur family stayed in Union Village for five years, long enough for Chet, as Chester was known, to attend the local academy for boys. Years later, a boyhood companion wrote of Chet at this time: "You might see him in the village street after a shower, watching boys building a mud dam across the rivulet in the roadway. Pretty soon he would be ordering this one to bring stones, another sticks, and other sods and mud . . . and they would all do his bidding without question. But he took care not to get any of the dirt on his hands." It was as good a training as any for a boy who would one day direct the workings of a powerful political party.

In 1844 Elder Arthur moved his family once again, this time to the First Baptist Church parish in Schenectady, New York. Here Chet attended the Lyceum in preparation for entering nearby Union College, one of the most respected colleges of the day. It was as a student at the

Lawyer and statesman Henry Clay

Lyceum that fourteen-year-old Chet had his first taste of political brawling. A supporter of Henry Clay, the Whig Party's presidential candidate, Chet got into a fight with some young Clay opponents. Years later, President Arthur was to recall, "I have been in many a political battle since then, but none livelier, or that more thoroughly enlisted me."

Schenectady, New York, where Arthur attended the Lyceum

After his preparatory work at the Lyceum, Chet entered Union College as a sophomore in September 1845. A classmate remembers him this way: "In disposition he was genial and very sociable, and he had a good relative standing in his class though not a very diligent student." The records show that Arthur took part in his share of college pranks and, to his father's displeasure, was fined several times for skipping chapel. Still, he found time to make the

Union College

Phi Beta Kappa academic fraternity, and serve as president of the debating society. And he did all this while teaching school during vacations to help pay his expenses!

Graduation exercises were held in July 1848, when Chester Arthur gave an address entitled "The Destiny of Genius." Then it was off into the real world—the world of the recent Mexican War, the California Gold Rush, and the increasing controversy over slavery.

In the mid-nineteenth century, railroads were rapidly expanding across the the eastern United States and extending to the West.

Chapter 3

A Young Lawyer in New York

After graduating from Union College, Arthur continued to teach while studying law in his spare time. By 1853 he had saved enough money from his $35-a-month salary to travel to New York City. Here he served as clerk in the law office of E. D. Culver, an abolitionist lawyer the Arthurs had known from Union Village days. After a year of clerking and further study, Arthur was admitted to the bar in May 1854 and made a partner in the firm then called Culver, Parker, and Arthur.

The mid-nineteenth century was a prosperous time for the United States. Its boundaries stretched from the Atlantic to the Pacific Ocean. With a population of over twenty-three million, it had more citizens than Great Britain. Immigrants flooded the country from Ireland, Germany, The Netherlands, and Great Britain, enticed by the promise of free land, a democratic government, and California gold. Railroads were rapidly expanding across the eastern part of the country, while telegraph lines connected New York and Chicago. American cotton was prized around the world, and U.S. clipper ships were the fastest and most graceful on the seas.

Above: German emigrants preparing to sail for America in the mid-1800s

Left: An 1848 booklet claiming to give foreign emigrants a complete guide for gold digging in the California gold mines

Above: The American clipper ship *Dreadnaught* on the high seas
Below: Black slaves gathering and processing cotton in the South

Burning abolitionist documents in Charleston, South Carolina

But beneath all this prosperity, the slavery issue still festered, and the question of black people's rights remained unresolved. As a young lawyer, Chester Arthur was directly involved in two cases that addressed this question.

The first was the Lemmon Slave Case. Jonathon Lemmon had brought eight slaves into New York from Virginia in 1852. Abolitionists argued that, since New York state law did not allow slavery, the slaves should go free. The Lemmons replied that the slaves were just passing through New York and, as nonresidents of the free state, were not bound by its laws. The courts agreed with the abolitionists through three trials—right up to the New York court of appeals. Though no one knows precisely what role Chester Arthur played in the case, it is certain that he took an active part.

Arthur's exact role is known in the second case. Elizabeth Jennings was a black public school teacher who was forcibly ejected from a New York streetcar in July 1854. Arthur took her case to trial and won a judgment against the streetcar company for $250 plus court costs. As a direct result of this case, all New York City public transportation was integrated. Elder Arthur would have been proud of his boy!

It was about this time that Arthur first became involved with politics. He had been a Whig ever since his involvement as a schoolboy with the Henry Clay campaign of 1844. But the Whig Party had collapsed after 1852, and in 1854 Arthur attended a meeting that eventually led to the formation of the new, antislavery Republican Party in New York. Within two years he was serving as an inspector of election polling places and actively campaigning for Republican candidates.

In 1856 Arthur and a friend named Henry D. Gardiner formed their own law partnership. But before they set up practice, the two young men decided to see the West, perhaps even settle there permanently. Their destination was Kansas, which was currently embroiled in a war between free-state forces, each trying to claim the area for itself.

Arthur and Gardiner stayed three or four months in Kansas. By that time the tensions, threats of violence, and decreasing economic opportunities drove them home to New York.

Captain William Herndon upon his sinking ship

For Chester Arthur, there was another reason to hurry home. Shortly before leaving for Kansas, he had become engaged to a charming Virginia girl named Ellen Lewis Herndon, nicknamed Nell. While he was in Kansas, Nell's father, a heroic navy lieutenant and explorer, went down with his ship off Cape Hatteras, North Carolina. The heartbroken Nell wrote the news to Arthur, who hurried to her side and assumed all legal and financial responsibilities for her family. Two years later, on October 25, 1859, Ellen Herndon and Chester Arthur were married and set up housekeeping in New York City.

Opposite page: Ellen Herndon

Chapter 4

General Arthur

Once settled in New York with Nell, Arthur turned again to the practice of law. For a young lawyer without family connections, a healthy bank account, or a large circle of influential friends, it was difficult to build up a lucrative practice in such a competitive city. Arthur was shrewd enough to realize that, since he didn't have powerful family connections or much money, it was up to him to develop influential friends. And the quickest way to do this was through politics.

Politics suited the young lawyer. Besides helping build up his law practice, it allowed him to develop the social side of his character. He liked mingling with important men, he liked wining and dining and dressing well, and he liked playing the game of getting political power.

These were the years when a man named Thurlow Weed controlled New York politics. Often referred to as The Dictator, Weed was an excellent teacher in the workings of party politics. He had ballot boxes stuffed with extra votes. He discouraged voters from voting for opposition candidates—using physical force if necessary. He supported the

New York political boss Thurlow Weed

"spoils system" — that is, he rewarded loyal party workers with government jobs, whether or not they were the best people for those jobs. In return, Weed demanded "voluntary contributions." In reality, a certain percentage of their salaries went back into the party pot and ensured Weed's continued authority. Weed was "honest" in his way — he was never caught taking bribes and didn't run his machine simply to make himself rich — but he shamefully manipulated the democratic process.

This was the man Chester Arthur had as a political tutor. Arthur first caught Weed's eye when he helped reelect Republican Edwin D. Morgan as governor of New York in 1860. In return, Weed recommended Arthur to

Governor Morgan. In addition to entering politics, Arthur had joined the state militia on his return to New York. So Morgan appointed the young lawyer as engineer-in-chief on his military staff.

At the age of thirty, Chester Arthur found himself in a position exactly suited to his tastes and abilities. He still practiced law, though not too diligently. He was a favorite of the powerful Republican governor of the nation's most populous state. His duties as engineer-in-chief mainly consisted of showing off his expensive, gaudy uniform at numerous social occasions. He had a beautiful wife with whom he was deeply in love—and a brand-new baby boy on whom they doted. Life was good—and then, in April of 1861, Confederate shells burst on the Union flag at Fort Sumter, in South Carolina, and the Civil War began.

Suddenly, Chester Arthur's ceremonial position of engineer-in-chief became a real job. With the rank of brigadier general, he was assigned to the quartermaster general's office in New York City. Here his industry, reliability, and good judgment soon earned him the title of acting assistant quartermaster general.

Arthur's job was to feed, clothe, shelter, and equip the thousands of men who rushed to enlist in the New York state militia. Then, since New York was the jumping-off point for war-bound soldiers from all over New England, he also had to feed and shelter these additional thousands of men who flooded the city from other states. There were no directions to guide him in his duties, no rulebook to show the way. Everything was being done for the first time, but it had to be done right—and done right away.

Above: Federal troops defending Fort Sumter from Confederate attack
Below: A regiment of Union troops headed for Washington, D.C.

Civil War troops in their camp in Staten Island, New York

General Arthur's success in meeting this new challenge may have surprised even himself. Setting up his own business systems as he went along, he soon had matters under control. He housed soldiers in private quarters until emergency barracks could be built. He managed unruly troops and soothed the citizens whose feathers they sometimes ruffled. He issued contracts for food, uniforms, and equipment to the lowest bidders. Then he personally inspected everything from wool stockings to fresh vegetables to make sure the quality was right. It was a job that offered ample opportunity for favoritism, but Arthur's honesty earned him the respect of all who worked for him.

It earned him promotions, too. In February 1862 Arthur was named inspector general, and in July of the same year was made quartermaster general.

Battle between the Union *Monitor* and the Confederate *Merrimack*

Arthur's responsibilities increased throughout the war, and his duties varied from month to month. He inspected forts throughout New York and suggested ways of improving the state's defenses. He traveled out of state, too, visiting the South to inspect the New York troops he had outfitted. When the Confederate steamer *Merrimack* threatened to attack New York City, he met with engineers and military advisers to devise a plan to protect the harbor. Arthur also simplified enlistment procedures and improved living conditions for new recruits by establishing camps in each of the state's thirty-two senatorial districts. Then, through special contracts with the railroads to take troops to the front, he saved the federal government over $43,000.

All in all, Arthur's years in the quartermaster general's office were marked by energy, honesty, and industry. When Governor Morgan left office in 1863 and Arthur was relieved of his responsibilities, his successor had this to say:

"I found . . . a well organized system of labor and accountability, for which the State is chiefly indebted to . . . General Chester A. Arthur, who, by his practical good sense and unremitting exertion, at a period when everything was in confusion, reduced the operations of this department to a matured plan, by which large amounts of money were saved to the government, and great economy of time secured in carrying out the details of the same."

Later, Governor Morgan would recall: "He was my chief reliance in the duties of equipping and transporting troops and munitions of war . . . he displayed not only great executive ability and unbending integrity, but great knowledge of Army Regulations. He can say No (which is important) without giving offence."

And Arthur's son, who perhaps knew his father best, told an interviewer in 1931: "I think my father's greatest work was as Quartermaster General of New York State."

Arthur left the quartermaster general's office a poorer man than when he had entered it. Thus his main goal in the mid-1860s was, quite frankly, to make money. He and Nell loved gracious living; they entertained often and well. And, as ambitious members of New York's high society, they were expected to live in a fine house and employ numerous servants.

Richmond, Virginia, in ruins at the end of the Civil War

So Arthur immediately set to work rebuilding his law practice. With his new political and military connections, he soon developed a specialty for handling war claims. It often seemed that he spent as much time in Washington, D.C., as in New York.

He used his political connections in another way, too. Nell came from a family of southerners, and she was concerned about her Confederate relatives' well-being. Whenever possible, Arthur interceded on his in-laws' behalf. This included visiting them on his trips south when he was quartermaster general, negotiating to spare family homesteads during military campaigns, and visiting captured Herndon family soldiers in Union prisoner-of-war camps. Like countless other families, the Arthurs had divided loyalties throughout the Civil War.

Above: Richmond on the morning of April 2, 1865, before it was burned
Below: Part of Richmond after it was burned by Union forces

Robert E. Lee surrenders to Ulysses S. Grant

Along with the national tragedy of the Civil War, Chester and Nell Arthur suffered a personal tragedy on July 8, 1863. While the rest of the nation mourned the more than 50,000 Union and Confederate soldiers killed, wounded, or missing in the great battle at Gettysburg, Pennsylvania, on July 1-3, Chester wrote in a letter to his brother: "I have sad, sad news to tell you. We have lost our darling boy. He died yesterday morning at Englewood, N.J., where we are staying for a few weeks—from convulsions, brought on by some affection of the brain. It came upon us so unexpectedly and suddenly. Nell is broken

The assassination of Abraham Lincoln

hearted. I fear much for her health. You know how her heart was wrapped up in her dear boy."

Slowly, tragically, the Civil War ground to a halt. On April 9, 1865, Confederate general Robert E. Lee surrendered to Union general Ulysses S. Grant in Appomattox Court House, Virginia. Five days later, John Wilkes Booth shot and killed President Abraham Lincoln as he sat watching a play in Ford's Theater in Washington, D.C. It was left to now-president Andrew Johnson to heal old wounds and bring North and South together as one Union again.

Chapter 5

The Man and the Machine

The years following the Civil War were chaotic ones in the United States. In the South, thousands of homeless white citizens and newly freed slaves tried to build lives for themselves out of the ruins left by war. For the federal government, Reconstruction was the issue. This was the government's plan for rebuilding the South after the War. President Johnson, a southern Democrat, favored Lincoln's Reconstruction policies of going easy on the renegade Confederate states. He wanted to give the white South a chance to rebuild itself economically. However, he showed little interest in securing civil rights for the former slaves.

Opposing him were the radical Republicans, who favored strong civil rights for blacks and severe punishment for the southern states. The congressional elections of 1866 gave the radicals an overwhelming victory. This paved the way for harsh treatment of the South, the gradual decline in power for conservative Republicans—and the eventual impeachment of President Andrew Johnson in 1868.

Above: President Johnson is served with his impeachment summons.
Below: The impeachment trial of Andrew Johnson in the Senate chamber

One of the leaders of the radical Republicans was a newly elected senator from New York State, the colorful and persuasive Roscoe Conkling. Conkling liked power, and he realized that a divided party could wield no real power. Hence, he set out to woo conservative leaders, and one of his first converts was Chester A. Arthur.

It was through his association with Conkling that Arthur really began to work hard at playing the game of politics. He was a behind-the-scenes organizer, working with Conkling to establish one of the most efficient political machines that New York State had ever seen. It was a machine based largely on the spoils system, whereby men who worked for the party and paid their dues got the best government jobs available. Conkling's power came from his control over federal job appointments. He produced the votes to elect the candidates, and in return the elected officials offered federal jobs to Conkling's workers.

By 1868 Roscoe Conkling and his band of followers, called Stalwarts, were firmly in power. Arthur was chairman of the state Republican executive committee, Conkling was head of the New York Republican machine, and Ulysses S. Grant—the Stalwart Republican candidate—was newly elected as president of the United States.

President Grant understood the spoils system perhaps better than anyone. After his inauguration, he lost no time in thanking Conkling for delivering the votes. He showed his gratitude by handing out a great number of government jobs to his Stalwart supporters. By 1871, in fact, there were so many of these "spoilsmen" in federal jobs that the public began to protest.

Above: President Ulysses S. Grant
Below: President Grant's cabinet in session

The New York Custom House

One of the worst dens of corruption was the New York Custom House. Employing over a thousand people, the Custom House was the nation's largest federal employer. Since there was no system of civil service examinations for filling government jobs, the employees were picked by the political party in power. Often, a jobholder's only qualification was the number of votes he had managed to bring out at the last election. Once in the custom house, each employee paid part of his salary back into his party's campaign fund. It was no wonder that custom house employees put themselves and their party ahead of their job responsibilities. Likewise, it was no wonder that the employee turnover at the custom house was so enormous. As one president came into the White House, his spoilsmen would replace those of the previous administration.

Roscoe Conkling shows what he considers to be a good Republican.

The custom house offered other opportunities for corruption as well. Officially, the custom house was to collect taxes on all goods that came into the Port of New York and to collect fines for customs violations. These fees were then to be paid into the federal treasury. However, there were plenty of ways that dishonest employees could skim a little profit off the top—for themselves, or for their party's treasury.

The public outcry against such thievery forced President Grant to demand the resignation of his first choice for collector of the Port of New York, Thomas Murphy, in 1871. Many Conkling Republicans were sad to see Murphy go—he had served his party well. But their disappoint-

The Port of New York at the time Chester Arthur was customs collector

ment did not last long, as Grant then turned to Chester Arthur as his next choice for this prized job.

On November 21, 1871, Chester A. Arthur was named collector of customs for the Port of New York. It was a momentous day for him. Even as the announcement of his appointment was being made public, another announcement was going out—on the birth of the Arthurs' new daughter. Chester and Nell were delighted as baby Ellen joined the son, Alan, who had been born to them in 1864. A happy home, two healthy children—and now the highest paying, most responsible appointment in the federal government. Chet Arthur had every reason to feel pleased with the way his life was going.

Chapter 6

The Custom House

As collector of customs for the Port of New York, Chester A. Arthur was in a very powerful position. The New York Custom House was the largest in the nation. It collected about 75 percent of the country's customs fees. During Arthur's six-year stint, those fees amounted to over $860,000,000!

Arthur's own salary was nothing to scoff at, either. During his first three years as collector, he was given a percentage of the fines and penalties he collected, making an average annual salary of over $50,000 — as much as the president himself earned! Unfortunately for Arthur, this percentage system was abolished in 1874. After that, the collector received a straight salary of only $12,000 — a severe drop for a man who enjoyed living well.

Still, both Nell and Chester were delighted with Arthur's job at the custom house. It established them as one of the most influential couples in New York. Nell loved the entertaining and social life that came with her husband's position — even if she sometimes resented the long hours he spent away from home.

A "memorial" to the spoils system

The demands on Arthur as collector were great, and he gave generously of his time. He was a popular collector — tactful, sophisticated, and businesslike — and he got along equally well with equals and subordinates. Still, most of his time was devoted to machine politics. On a typical day, he showed up at the office in the early afternoon, worked for several hours, and then set out for an evening of entertainment. Perhaps he would have dinner and attend an opera with Nell and then spend hours eating, drinking, and smoking cigars with the "boys" of the Conkling

President Grant holds a reception for Indians at the White House.

machine. He never forgot where his loyalties lay, and he
made no attempt to hide his party affiliation.

Arthur continued happily in this manner for several
years. Meanwhile, President Grant's Republican administration continued to be riddled with corruption. People
throughout the state, and indeed all around the country,
were getting fed up with what they saw as a Republican
problem. In reaction, New York State elected a Democratic
governor in 1874. It was the beginning of the end of the
Conkling machine.

President Rutherford B. Hayes

The crumbling of Conkling's Republican power base worsened during the presidential elections of 1876. When Rutherford B. Hayes entered the White House, it was a reform Republican who was taking office, not a Conkling Stalwart.

On becoming president, one of Hayes's first acts was to issue an order forbidding federal employees "to take part in the management of political organizations, caucuses, conventions, or election campaigns." This same order also put an end to the practice of handing over part of one's salary to one's political party. These two orders, if put into effect, would spell death to the Conkling machine. His next act was aimed even more pointedly at the Conkling machine—he appointed a commission to investigate corruption in the New York Custom House.

Everyone agreed that the investigation wasn't aimed directly at Chester Arthur. It was true that he made

Federal job applicants take the new civil service exams.

appointments according to party membership, that his list of employees was far too long, and that he encouraged the practice of assessing salaries. Then, too, his role as Conkling's chief lieutenant in the Republican Party was no secret. But on the whole, Arthur had fulfilled the office of collector efficiently and well. Certainly no one accused him of personally profiting from his position.

But reform was in the air, and reformers saw the investigation as a way of further weakening Conkling's machine. The commission's report came back with bad news for Arthur: there was corruption and waste in custom house business, and continued party involvement by custom house officials. Though Arthur and Conkling fought it as best they could, in the end Hayes and his reformers got their way. By July 1878, Chester A. Arthur's six-year stint as collector of customs of the Port of New York was over.

CHESTER A. ARTHUR.

Chapter 7

The Vice-Presidency

Once again, Chester Arthur returned to his private law practice. But his heart wasn't in it, and more and more he found himself actively involved with the affairs of the Republican Party. Conkling's machine had received a serious blow from the custom house fiasco, but it hadn't been knocked completely out of commission. The new drive was to get Hayes and his reformers out of the White House in the upcoming 1880 elections. And in his place? A third term for former president Ulysses S. Grant!

As permanent president of New York's Republican central committee, Chester Arthur was at the center of the statewide campaign. He worked tirelessly throughout New York, furthering Republican causes as only he knew how. But though he and the other Conkling supporters did their best, when the Republican national convention rolled around in July 1880, they were unable to win the nomination for Grant. Instead, on the thirty-sixth ballot, the vote went to reformer James A. Garfield of Ohio.

Levi P. Morton, who refused the vice-presidential nomination

Conkling was furious, and Garfield's backers knew it. They also knew that they would need Conkling's support if their candidate was to win the national election. So they did the politically tactful thing—they offered the vice-presidential nomination to a Stalwart.

Their first choice, a New Yorker named Levi P. Morton, turned down the nomination on the advice of the still-furious Conkling. Garfield's men then turned to Chester Arthur. Would he consider running for vice-president?

It wasn't a completely new idea to Arthur. Always the politician, he had already considered what he would do if the nomination were offered to him. Becoming vice-president would certainly help remove the sting of being sus-

James A. Garfield

pended from the custom house. Then, too, if Conkling's machine really was weakening, it wouldn't hurt to start establishing another power base for himself. Without hesitation, Arthur accepted the nomination.

But when he told Conkling that he had been offered the vice-presidency, the senator was scornful. "Well, sir," Conkling shot back, "you should drop it as you would a red hot shoe from the forge." He went on to warn Arthur of his conviction that Garfield could never win. But Arthur didn't budge. "The office of the Vice-President is a greater honor than I ever dreamed of attaining," he said firmly. "A barren nomination would be a great honor. In a calmer moment you will look at this differently."

Garfield and Arthur campaigning in New York City

Conkling disagreed. "If you wish for my favor and respect," he retorted, "you will contemptuously decline it."

By now Arthur was tired of the conversation. He would have liked to accept the vice-presidential nomination with Conkling's approval. But if that approval wasn't forthcoming, he would simply do without it. "Senator Conkling," he said with dignity, "I shall accept the nomination and I shall carry with me the majority of the delegation."

And he did, too. When he returned home, it was official: James A. Garfield was the Republican nominee for president, with Chester A. Arthur of New York as his running mate. It should have been a glorious moment for Arthur. The vice-presidency was within his grasp, and 2,500 loyal New York City Republicans were gathered in front of his hotel to cheer him on.

Arthur addressing a crowd in Albany, New York

But the one supporter whose cheers would have meant the most wasn't present. Exactly six months before, on January 12, 1880, Arthur's beloved Nell had succumbed to pneumonia. His wife and helpmate of over twenty years was gone. It was a crushing blow to Arthur, and he never got over regretting how different his life would have been had she lived. "Honors to me now," he confided sorrowfully to a friend, "are not what they once were."

As always, however, the best cure for whatever ailed Chester was vigorous political activity. Arthur knew that he didn't have the full support of his own party as he sought the vice-presidency. Liberal Republicans were appalled that their reform candidate for president should have as a running mate a man who openly sneered at civil service reform, calling it "snivel service."

Nation magazine editor Edward Lawrence Godkin

And Arthur certainly didn't have public opinion on his side. Already people were asking if they could vote for Garfield without also voting for Arthur. As editor E. L. Godkin of the *Nation* magazine commented wryly, "There is no place in which his powers of mischief will be so small as in the Vice Presidency. . . . It is true General Garfield, if elected, may die during his term of office, but this is too unlikely a contingency to be worth making extraordinary provision for." Little did he suspect how soon his words would come back to haunt him!

The only answer to these doubts was hard, shrewd political canvassing, and Arthur threw himself into the campaign with his usual vigor. He silenced some of his critics by endorsing civil service reform in his letter of accep-

Outgoing president Rutherford B. Hayes (right)

tance. He won over others through his tireless campaigning in key states. As the *New York Times* commented, "he has worked for weeks with such application as few men are capable of . . . and has seen several men about him laid up with fatigue while he has been compelled to keep right on. It would inspire Republicans with enthusiasm to see with what industry and judgment he goes on. . . ."

The hard work was worth it. The November election of 1880 brought out 78.4 percent of qualified voters, the largest percentage ever recorded in a presidential election. With over ten million ballots cast, Garfield and Arthur took the popular vote by a margin of just 7,018. It was a narrow victory—but a victory all the same!

Chapter 8

President Arthur

By 1880 the United States was in the midst of unprecedented economic growth. Westward expansion had opened up millions of acres of virgin farmland, and agricultural output was at an all-time high. Railroads and canals crisscrossed the country, making it easy to transport cotton, corn, and wheat throughout the nation and then out to the rest of the world.

Technology was booming, too. Alexander Graham Bell had patented the telephone, Thomas Edison had formed an electric light company, and Andrew Carnegie was cranking up his first steel mills. It was the beginning of what was called the Gilded Age in American history, when profits were great and "millionaire" was becoming a household word.

Vice-President Chester Arthur moved through this world with ease. Educated, sophisticated, and charming, he was the perfect example of the "gentleman boss."

Opposite page: Arthur becomes president.

Above: Alexander Graham Bell speaks into his telephone.
Below: The first telephone

Above: Inventor Thomas Edison in his laboratory
Below: Andrew Carnegie (center) at a tunnel for one of his railroads

A cartoon depicting
the brutal practice
of assessing the
salaries of New York
Custom House employees

Unfortunately, nobody really wanted a political boss as vice-president, even one who was a gentleman. But Arthur did nothing to change his image. Both before and after his inauguration he made it clear that he and Roscoe Conkling had long since made up any quarrel they may have had. Chester Arthur might be James Garfield's vice-president, but he was still first and foremost a key player on Roscoe Conkling's Stalwart team.

What did he do to show this? He openly campaigned for Conkling candidates—unsuitable behavior for a vice-president. In appointment disputes between Garfield and Conkling, he sided with Conkling instead of the president. He reversed his earlier position and again scorned the civil service reform movement. And he joked in public about the money spent to "buy" a Republican victory in Indiana during the presidential election.

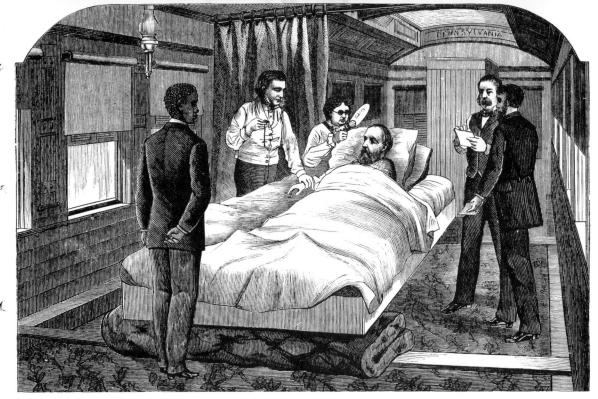

Garfield's ride from Washington, D.C., to Elberon, New Jersey

Then came the fateful day in July 1881, when President Garfield was shot in the Baltimore and Potomac railroad station in Washington, D.C. Public emotion ran high, and citizens were torn between feeling horrified at what had happened to the president and at what would happen to the country if Arthur should become president.

It didn't help matters that Garfield's assassin, Charles Guiteau, was a disappointed office-seeker. Guiteau was almost a joke around Washington. He had supported the Garfield-Arthur ticket during the campaign and afterwards had pestered anyone he could find to make him ambassador to Austria. Frustrated and more than a little bit insane, Guiteau had finally settled on assassination as the solution to his problems. Guiteau's actions convinced the nation that, regardless of the vice-president's feelings, civil service reform was long overdue.

Throughout the long, hot summer President Garfield fought for his life. In New York, Vice-President Arthur struggled to remain calm, his private anxiety so great that friends worried for his health. But in public Arthur behaved with dignity and composure, impressing even the most skeptical of observers. By the time Garfield died on September 19, 1881, most of the American public was prepared to give Chester A. Arthur the benefit of the doubt as he stepped into his new role as president. As the *New York Sun* declared: "While Mr. Arthur is not a man who would have entered anybody's mind as a direct candidate for the office, it is not at all certain that he will not make a successful administration. He is a gentleman in his manners ... his bearing is manly. ... Truth in speech and fidelity to his friends and his engagements form a part of his character. He has tact and common sense."

President Arthur assumed his new command quietly enough. He was sworn into office in New York by state supreme court judge John R. Brady the night Garfield died. This oath was repeated on September 22 before U.S. Supreme Court chief justice Waite at the Capitol in Washington. A brief, solemn inaugural speech followed: " ... All the noble aspirations of my lamented predecessor ... to correct abuses, to enforce economy, to advance prosperity, and to promote the general welfare, to insure domestic security and maintain friendly and honorable relations with the nations of the earth, will be garnered in the hearts of the people, and it will be my earnest endeavor to profit, and to see that the nation shall profit, by his example and experience. ... Summoned to

President Arthur tempted by a host of corruptions

these high duties and responsibilities . . . I assume the trust imposed by the Constitution, relying for aid on divine guidance and the virtue, patriotism, and intelligence of the American people."

Then it was down to work. In selecting his cabinet, President Arthur gave the first indication that he would not be merely a pawn in Roscoe Conkling's hands. Though Arthur did choose several trusted Stalwart associates to fill key spots, he flatly refused to give Conkling himself the desired post of secretary of state. (He did later offer him a seat on the Supreme Court, but Conkling, hurt, refused.) Instead, Arthur strove for a balanced cabinet that would serve no single faction.

The next order of business was the trial of Charles Guiteau. Though the nation called out for Guiteau's blood, Arthur was determined that the man be given a fair trial. Fair it was, but also something of a public circus. To nobody's surprise, Guiteau was found guilty and sentenced to hang on June 30, 1882.

Next Arthur turned to the investigation, begun under Garfield, of the so-called Star Route Frauds. These post office frauds involved huge amounts of money paid for delivering mail to thinly populated regions of the West. When it was discovered that many of these routes didn't exist, Garfield had ordered the postmaster general to investigate.

Now Arthur pressed forward with this investigation, over the loud protests of his fellow Republicans. To the embarrassment of their party, two prominent Stalwarts, Stephen Dorsey and Thomas Brady, were found responsible for the frauds and were eventually brought to trial. But though Arthur urged the attorney general to prosecute "with the utmost vigor of the law," in the end the two defendants were found innocent.

Next Arthur turned to civil service reform. When he called for reform in his first annual message to Congress in December 1881, Congress ignored him. But the voters were on Arthur's side. With the memory of Charles Guiteau still fresh in their minds, they overturned Republican control of the House in the 1882 congressional elections.

Arthur again urged reform in his second annual address, and this time Congress responded. To the disgust of Conkling and his former Stalwart associates, Chester Arthur, former spoilsman, signed the Pendleton Act into law on January 16, 1883. This law established a three-man Civil Service Commission and set up a merit system for making federal job appointments. Examinations were required, and officials who demanded salary kickbacks were fined. It was the beginning of the end of the spoils system in federal government.

There was other business to attend to, too. Because of high tariffs and taxes, the U.S. Treasury had a surplus of some eighty to one hundred million dollars a year. This was money that sat in the treasury, out of circulation, instead of being spent by consumers to boost the U.S. economy.

To get rid of this surplus, Arthur proposed reducing tariffs and appointed a commission in 1882 to study the issue. The commission agreed with Arthur, but Congress ignored their recommendations for sharp tariff cuts. Instead, in 1883, Congress passed a law that lowered rates only a little—a reduction that was not nearly enough to do away with the surplus.

Congress had its own ideas of what to do with all that extra money. In 1882, it passed an $18,000,000 rivers and harbors bill to improve the nation's waterways. Arthur knew the bill was extravagant. He also knew that it offered too many opportunities for dishonest politicians to line their own wallets. So he vetoed the bill, over the loud protests of his own Republican Party.

But again Congress had its way, passing the bill over the president's veto.

Above: Reporters interviewing Charles Guiteau in jail
Below: A cartoon on the Star Route Frauds

Above: A cartoon captioned, "King Arthur and His Round Table"
Below: A cartoon on the 1882 congressional elections

Another issue for which Arthur fought long and hard was the U.S. Navy. America's naval forces had deteriorated since the Civil War twenty years earlier. Now Arthur feared that its ships and equipment were too old and outdated to be of much use in any battle at sea. As a British journal commented, "Never was there such a hopeless, broken-down, tattered, forlorn apology for a navy."

Arthur argued the navy's case in both of his annual addresses, and in 1883 Congress finally approved the construction of three new steel cruisers and a dispatch boat. Though their production was plagued by delays, fire, and deliveries of inferior materials, the ships were finally completed. And despite construction problems, they turned out to be superbly built. These ships marked the beginning of a naval modernization that continued through the 1898 Spanish-American War and beyond.

Arthur also presided over the first federal law restricting immigration. On August 3, 1882, Congress passed a law that established a tax of fifty cents per immigrant. This same law barred entrance to "undesirables" — convicts, the insane, and paupers. It was passed mainly in response to public concern over the flood of immigrants pouring into America. Between 1881 and 1890, the new arrivals numbered over 5,000,000!

Though Chester Arthur had a busy enough time of it as president, it can't be said that he overworked himself. He arrived for work late, frequently left early, and was rarely on time for meetings. As one White House clerk confided, "President Arthur never did today what he could put off until tomorrow."

If Arthur found the official duties of being president tiresome, he loved the social obligations. He began fulfilling these obligations early in his term by renovating the White House. Before moving in, Arthur had some twenty-four wagonloads of furnishings (including priceless antiques from the eighteenth century) carted off to be sold at public auction. Then he hired Louis C. Tiffany, the famed designer of stained glass, to redecorate the White House in grand Victorian style—including such modern innovations as an elevator and indoor plumbing.

Arthur finally moved into the White House in December 1881. With him came his youngest sister, Mary Arthur McElroy, who had agreed to take the duties of First Lady and act as his Washington hostess. Between them, they raised social life at the White House to a peak of elegance and generosity unlike anything Washington had ever known. State dinners were served in twenty-one courses, each course lovingly prepared by Arthur's hand-chosen French chef. Floral centerpieces ran over five feet long and two feet high, with the florist bill for one dinner coming to $1,500. Fine wine and frequent music became the norm, and formal evening wear the rule.

President Arthur was a familiar and popular sight on the streets of Washington as well as inside the White House. With a flower in his buttonhole and a silk handkerchief in his vest pocket, he had a nod and a bow for all who greeted him. "It is not that he is handsome and agreeable—for he was both long ago," wrote one admirer, "but it is his ease, polish and perfect manner that make him the greatest society lion we have had in many years."

Arthur with his daughter, Nell, at home in the White House

President Arthur was a family man, too. Determined to give his children as normal a life as possible, he carefully shielded nine-year-old Nell and sixteen-year-old Alan from the fierce glare of Washington publicity. And of course, since he was a highly eligible bachelor, there were always rumors of a presidential romance. Interest ran high when it was learned that fresh flowers were placed daily before a woman's photograph in the White House. But even the most notorious gossips were silenced when they found that the photograph was of Arthur's late wife, Nell.

Arthur (center) on his trip to Yellowstone National Park

State dinners and receptions were not the only recreation Arthur enjoyed. He was considered one of the finest fishermen in America and took time off for outdoor vacations whenever his schedule allowed. The most famous of these vacations came in the summer of 1883. Accompanied by personal friends, various high-ranking army officers, seventy-five cavalry troopers, Indian guides, a photographer, and 175 pack animals, he made a grand tour of Yellowstone National Park. The highlight of the trip came when a Wyoming mountain peak was named in his honor.

Above: An 1884 cartoon on civil service reform
Below: The rough waters of Arthur's administration

Above: Roscoe Conkling sheds his fake political plumage.
Below: Arthur's political luck runs out.

Arthur, on vacation, along Bellevue Avenue in Newport, Rhode Island

But official and social obligations were taking their toll on the chief executive. In addition to the normal stresses of the job, Arthur carried with him the secret knowledge that he was seriously ill with what would later be diagnosed as Bright's disease, a fatal kidney ailment. Though he was frequently racked by pain, he refused to make his condition known. More and more, the image he projected of genial ease was just that—an image designed to deceive his public. Pain-ridden he might be, but an invalid—never!

Arthur lunching with a friend

By the fall of 1883, Republicans were looking ahead to possible candidates for the 1884 presidential elections. Arthur knew that he had virtually no chance of being named the Republican nominee. His support of civil service reform, his vigorous prosecution of fellow Republicans in the Star Route Frauds, and his unpopular veto of Congress's waterways bill had cost him the support of his party. Even his one-time mentor had turned against him. "I have but one annoyance with the Administration of President Arthur," Roscoe Conkling sneered, "and that is, that in contrast with it, the Administration of Hayes becomes respectable, if not heroic."

Unsuccessful Republican candidate James G. Blaine

Then, of course, there was the matter of Arthur's health. He knew he wasn't strong enough to run for or serve through another term as president. Still, not wanting to be thought fearful of defeat, he took the official position that he would welcome reelection. Privately, however, he urged his supporters not to attend the Republican convention on his behalf. As he told one avid delegate, "I do not want to be re-elected. Go to your friends and get them to stop their activities."

And so Chester Arthur left the political arena. James G. Blaine won the Republican nomination in June 1884 and then lost the national election to Democrat Grover Cleveland in November. The Republicans were out of the White House, and Chester Arthur was out of politics.

Above: Arthur as he is about to leave office
Below: Grover Cleveland is sworn in as president.

Chapter 9

Career's End

When Chester Arthur retired from the White House on March 4, 1885, he was asked about his plans for the future. "Well," he said wryly, "there doesn't seem anything else for an ex-President to do but to go into the country and raise big pumpkins."

Though Arthur went to New York City and not the country, his retirement was a quiet one. Poor health didn't permit him to return to the practice of law as he had hoped, and he spent most of his time at home on Lexington Avenue. And though well-meaning friends tried to persuade him to run for the New York State senate, he quietly but firmly rejected all such suggestions.

Gradually his condition worsened, and by February 1886, the doctors recognized that the Bright's disease had also brought about a serious heart condition. Now it was just a matter of time for Chester Arthur.

On November 18, 1886, barely twenty months since he left the office of president, Chester Arthur breathed his last. Surrounded by his children and devoted sisters, he had finally succumbed to a massive cerebral hemorrhage.

Chester A. Arthur was not one of the nation's strongest presidents. But despite the fears that accompanied him into the White House, neither was he one of the worst. He came into power at a time in American history when political parties existed mainly as what one historian has called "mercenary armies." Their major functions were winning elections, getting jobs, and doing favors. Ideals, ethics, party platforms—those were only of secondary importance.

Into this arena came Chester Arthur—well educated, dignified, charming, and with a flair for organization. He was the ideal party politician—the gentleman boss. His manipulation of the spoils system was unsurpassed, yet when tragic circumstances thrust him reluctantly into the presidency, he left all that behind him. As one of his former associates said sadly, "He isn't Chet Arthur any more—he's the President."

Arthur's attempts to be an honest president lost him whatever support he had had within his own party. Reformers didn't believe his transformation was real; members of the Stalwart machine couldn't believe their old friend would "turn" on them this way.

But the public treated Arthur a bit more kindly. Grateful for the dignity and calm he brought to the chaotic days following Garfield's shooting and death, they appreciated his efforts to serve his country honestly. As the *New York World* said after his death in 1886, "No duty was neglected in his administration, and no adventurous project alarmed the nation. There was no scandal to make us ashamed while he was in office and none to be ripped up

Arthur's tomb in Albany Rural Cemetery, Albany, New York

when he went out of it. He earned and deserved the honest fame he possesses."

Or perhaps novelist and humorist Mark Twain said it better: "I am but one in 55,000,000; still, in the opinion of this one-fifty-five-millionth of the country's population, it would be hard to better President Arthur's Administration."

It's not a bad tribute to a man who had never wanted to be president in the first place.

Chester Arthur on his famous fishing trip

Chronology of American History

(Shaded area covers events in Chester A. Arthur's lifetime.)

About A.D. 982 — Eric the Red, born in Norway, reaches Greenland in one of the first European voyages to North America.

About 1000 — Leif Ericson (Eric the Red's son) leads what is thought to be the first European expedition to mainland North America; Leif probably lands in Canada.

1492 — Christopher Columbus, seeking a sea route from Spain to the Far East, discovers the New World.

1497 — John Cabot reaches Canada in the first English voyage to North America.

1513 — Ponce de Léon explores Florida in search of the fabled Fountain of Youth.

1519-1521 — Hernando Cortés of Spain conquers Mexico.

1534 — French explorers led by Jacques Cartier enter the Gulf of St. Lawrence in Canada.

1540 — Spanish explorer Francisco Coronado begins exploring the American Southwest, seeking the riches of the mythical Seven Cities of Cibola.

1565 — St. Augustine, Florida, the first permanent European town in what is now the United States, is founded by the Spanish.

1607 — Jamestown, Virginia, is founded, the first permanent English town in the present-day U.S.

1608 — Frenchman Samuel de Champlain founds the village of Quebec, Canada.

1609 — Henry Hudson explores the eastern coast of present-day U.S. for the Netherlands; the Dutch then claim parts of New York, New Jersey, Delaware, and Connecticut and name the area New Netherland.

1619 — The English colonies' first shipment of black slaves arrives in Jamestown.

1620 — English Pilgrims found Massachusetts' first permanent town at Plymouth.

1621 — Massachusetts Pilgrims and Indians hold the famous first Thanksgiving feast in colonial America.

1623 — Colonization of New Hampshire is begun by the English.

1624 — Colonization of present-day New York State is begun by the Dutch at Fort Orange (Albany).

1625 — The Dutch start building New Amsterdam (now New York City).

1630 — The town of Boston, Massachusetts, is founded by the English Puritans.

1633 — Colonization of Connecticut is begun by the English.

1634 — Colonization of Maryland is begun by the English.

1636 — Harvard, the colonies' first college, is founded in Massachusetts. Rhode Island colonization begins when Englishman Roger Williams founds Providence.

1638 — Delaware colonization begins as Swedes build Fort Christina at present-day Wilmington.

1640 — Stephen Daye of Cambridge, Massachusetts prints *The Bay Psalm Book*, the first English-language book published in what is now the U.S.

1643 — Swedish settlers begin colonizing Pennsylvania.

About 1650 — North Carolina is colonized by Virginia settlers.

1660 — New Jersey colonization is begun by the Dutch at present-day Jersey City.

1670 — South Carolina colonization is begun by the English near Charleston.

1673 — Jacques Marquette and Louis Jolliet explore the upper Mississippi River for France.

1682—Philadelphia, Pennsylvania, is settled. La Salle explores Mississippi River all the way to its mouth in Louisiana and claims the whole Mississippi Valley for France.

1693—College of William and Mary is founded in Williamsburg, Virginia.

1700—Colonial population is about 250,000.

1703—Benjamin Franklin is born in Boston.

1732—George Washington, first president of the U.S., is born in Westmoreland County, Virginia.

1733—James Oglethorpe founds Savannah, Georgia; Georgia is established as the thirteenth colony.

1735—John Adams, second president of the U.S., is born in Braintree, Massachusetts.

1737—William Byrd founds Richmond, Virginia.

1738—British troops are sent to Georgia over border dispute with Spain.

1739—Black insurrection takes place in South Carolina.

1740—English Parliament passes act allowing naturalization of immigrants to American colonies after seven-year residence.

1743—Thomas Jefferson is born in Albemarle County, Virginia. Benjamin Franklin retires at age thirty-seven to devote himself to scientific inquiries and public service.

1744—King George's War begins; France joins war effort against England.

1745—During King George's War, France raids settlements in Maine and New York.

1747—Classes begin at Princeton College in New Jersey.

1748—The Treaty of Aix-la-Chapelle concludes King George's War.

1749—Parliament legally recognizes slavery in colonies and the inauguration of the plantation system in the South. George Washington becomes the surveyor for Culpepper County in Virginia.

1750—Thomas Walker passes through and names Cumberland Gap on his way toward Kentucky region. Colonial population is about 1,200,000.

1751—James Madison, fourth president of the U.S., is born in Port Conway, Virginia. English Parliament passes Currency Act, banning New England colonies from issuing paper money. George Washington travels to Barbados.

1752—Pennsylvania Hospital, the first general hospital in the colonies, is founded in Philadelphia. Benjamin Franklin uses a kite in a thunderstorm to demonstrate that lightning is a form of electricity.

1753—George Washington delivers command that the French withdraw from the Ohio River Valley; French disregard the demand. Colonial population is about 1,328,000.

1754—French and Indian War begins (extends to Europe as the Seven Years' War). Washington surrenders at Fort Necessity.

1755—French and Indians ambush Braddock. Washington becomes commander of Virginia troops.

1756—England declares war on France.

1758—James Monroe, fifth president of the U.S., is born in Westmoreland County, Virginia.

1759—Cherokee Indian war begins in southern colonies; hostilities extend to 1761. George Washington marries Martha Dandridge Custis.

1760—George III becomes king of England. Colonial population is about 1,600,000.

1762—England declares war on Spain.

1763—Treaty of Paris concludes the French and Indian War and the Seven Years' War. England gains Canada and most other French lands east of the Mississippi River.

1764—British pass the Sugar Act to gain tax money from the colonists. The issue of taxation without representation is first introduced in Boston. John Adams marries Abigail Smith.

1765—Stamp Act goes into effect in the colonies. Business virtually stops as almost all colonists refuse to use the stamps.

1766—British repeal the Stamp Act.

1767—John Quincy Adams, sixth president of the U.S. and son of second president John Adams, is born in Braintree, Massachusetts. Andrew Jackson, seventh president of the U.S., is born in Waxhaw settlement, South Carolina.

1769—Daniel Boone sights the Kentucky Territory.

1770—In the Boston Massacre, British soldiers kill five colonists and injure six. Townshend Acts are repealed, thus eliminating all duties on imports to the colonies except tea.

1771—Benjamin Franklin begins his autobiography, a work that he will never complete. The North Carolina assembly passes the "Bloody Act," which makes rioters guilty of treason.

1772—Samuel Adams rouses colonists to consider British threats to self-government.

1773—English Parliament passes the Tea Act. Colonists dressed as Mohawk Indians board British tea ships and toss 342 casks of tea into the water in what becomes known as the Boston Tea Party. William Henry Harrison is born in Charles City County, Virginia.

1774—British close the port of Boston to punish the city for the Boston Tea Party. First Continental Congress convenes in Philadelphia.

1775—American Revolution begins with battles of Lexington and Concord, Massachusetts. Second Continental Congress opens in Philadelphia. George Washington becomes commander-in-chief of the Continental army.

1776—Declaration of Independence is adopted on July 4.

1777—Congress adopts the American flag with thirteen stars and thirteen stripes. John Adams is sent to France to negotiate peace treaty.

1778—France declares war against Great Britain and becomes U.S. ally.

1779—British surrender to Americans at Vincennes. Thomas Jefferson is elected governor of Virginia. James Madison is elected to the Continental Congress.

1780—Benedict Arnold, first American traitor, defects to the British.

1781—Articles of Confederation go into effect. Cornwallis surrenders to George Washington at Yorktown, ending the American Revolution.

1782—American commissioners, including John Adams, sign peace treaty with British in Paris. Thomas Jefferson's wife, Martha, dies. Martin Van Buren is born in Kinderhook, New York.

1784—Zachary Taylor is born near Barboursville, Virginia.

1785—Congress adopts the dollar as the unit of currency. John Adams is made minister to Great Britain. Thomas Jefferson is appointed minister to France.

1786—Shays's Rebellion begins in Massachusetts.

1787—Constitutional Convention assembles in Philadelphia, with George Washington presiding; U.S. Constitution is adopted. Delaware, New Jersey, and Pennsylvania become states.

1788—Virginia, South Carolina, New York, Connecticut, New Hampshire, Maryland, and Massachusetts become states. U.S. Constitution is ratified. New York City is declared U.S. capital.

1789—Presidential electors elect George Washington and John Adams as first president and vice-president. Thomas Jefferson is appointed secretary of state. North Carolina becomes a state. French Revolution begins.

1790—Supreme Court meets for the first time. Rhode Island becomes a state. First national census in the U.S. counts 3,929,214 persons. John Tyler is born in Charles City County, Virginia.

1791—Vermont enters the Union. U.S. Bill of Rights, the first ten amendments to the Constitution, goes into effect. District of Columbia is established. James Buchanan is born in Stony Batter, Pennsylvania.

1792—Thomas Paine publishes *The Rights of Man*. Kentucky becomes a state. Two political parties are formed in the U.S., Federalist and Republican. Washington is elected to a second term, with Adams as vice-president.

1793—War between France and Britain begins; U.S. declares neutrality. Eli Whitney invents the cotton gin; cotton production and slave labor increase in the South.

1794—Eleventh Amendment to the Constitution is passed, limiting federal courts' power. "Whiskey Rebellion" in Pennsylvania protests federal whiskey tax. James Madison marries Dolley Payne Todd.

1795—George Washington signs the Jay Treaty with Great Britain. Treaty of San Lorenzo, between U.S. and Spain, settles Florida boundary and gives U.S. right to navigate the Mississippi. James Polk is born near Pineville, North Carolina.

1796—Tennessee enters the Union. Washington gives his Farewell Address, refusing a third presidential term. John Adams is elected president and Thomas Jefferson vice-president.

1797—Adams recommends defense measures against possible war with France. Napoleon Bonaparte and his army march against Austrians in Italy. U.S. population is about 4,900,000.

1798—Washington is named commander-in-chief of the U.S. Army. Department of the Navy is created. Alien and Sedition Acts are passed. Napoleon's troops invade Egypt and Switzerland.

1799—George Washington dies at Mount Vernon, New York. James Monroe is elected governor of Virginia. French Revolution ends. Napoleon becomes ruler of France.

1800—Thomas Jefferson and Aaron Burr tie for president. U.S. capital is moved from Philadelphia to Washington, D.C. The White House is built as presidents' home. Spain returns Louisiana to France. Millard Fillmore is born in Locke, New York.

1801—After thirty-six ballots, House of Representatives elects Thomas Jefferson president, making Burr vice-president. James Madison is named secretary of state.

1802—Congress abolishes excise taxes. U.S. Military Academy is founded at West Point, New York.

1803—Ohio enters the Union. Louisiana Purchase treaty is signed with France, greatly expanding U.S. territory.

1804—Twelfth Amendment to the Constitution rules that president and vice-president be elected separately. Alexander Hamilton is killed by Vice-President Aaron Burr in a duel. Orleans Territory is established. Napoleon crowns himself emperor of France. Franklin Pierce is born in Hillsborough Lower Village, New Hampshire.

1805—Thomas Jefferson begins his second term as president. Lewis and Clark expedition reaches the Pacific Ocean.

1806—Coinage of silver dollars is stopped; resumes in 1836.

1807—Aaron Burr is acquitted in treason trial. Embargo Act closes U.S. ports to trade.

1808—James Madison is elected president. Congress outlaws importing slaves from Africa. Andrew Johnson is born in Raleigh, North Carolina.

1809—Abraham Lincoln is born near Hodgenville, Kentucky.

1810—U.S. population is 7,240,000.

1811—William Henry Harrison defeats Indians at Tippecanoe. Monroe is named secretary of state.

1812—Louisiana becomes a state. U.S. declares war on Britain (War of 1812). James Madison is reelected president. Napoleon invades Russia.

1813—British forces take Fort Niagara and Buffalo, New York.

1814—Francis Scott Key writes "The Star-Spangled Banner." British troops burn much of Washington, D.C., including the White House. Treaty of Ghent ends War of 1812. James Monroe becomes secretary of war.

1815—Napoleon meets his final defeat at Battle of Waterloo.

1816—James Monroe is elected president. Indiana becomes a state.

1817—Mississippi becomes a state. Construction on Erie Canal begins.

1818—Illinois enters the Union. The present thirteen-stripe flag is adopted. Border between U.S. and Canada is agreed upon.

1819—Alabama becomes a state. U.S. purchases Florida from Spain. Thomas Jefferson establishes the University of Virginia.

1820—James Monroe is reelected. In the Missouri Compromise, Maine enters the Union as a free (non-slave) state.

1821—Missouri enters the Union as a slave state. Santa Fe Trail opens the American Southwest. Mexico declares independence from Spain. Napoleon Bonaparte dies.

1822—U.S. recognizes Mexico and Colombia. Liberia in Africa is founded as a home for freed slaves. Ulysses S. Grant is born in Point Pleasant, Ohio. Rutherford B. Hayes is born in Delaware, Ohio.

1823—Monroe Doctrine closes North and South America to European colonizing or invasion.

1824—House of Representatives elects John Quincy Adams president when none of the four candidates wins a majority in national election. Mexico becomes a republic.

1825—Erie Canal is opened. U.S. population is 11,300,000.

1826—Thomas Jefferson and John Adams both die on July 4, the fiftieth anniversary of the Declaration of Independence.

1828—Andrew Jackson is elected president. Tariff of Abominations is passed, cutting imports.

1829—James Madison attends Virginia's constitutional convention. Slavery is abolished in Mexico. Chester A. Arthur is born in Fairfield, Vermont.

1830—Indian Removal Act to resettle Indians west of the Mississippi is approved.

1831—James Monroe dies in New York City. James A. Garfield is born in Orange, Ohio. Cyrus McCormick develops his reaper.

1832—Andrew Jackson, nominated by the new Democratic Party, is reelected president.

1833—Britain abolishes slavery in its colonies. Benjamin Harrison is born in North Bend, Ohio.

1835—Federal government becomes debt-free for the first time.

1836—Martin Van Buren becomes president. Texas wins independence from Mexico. Arkansas joins the Union. James Madison dies at Montpelier, Virginia.

1837—Michigan enters the Union. U.S. population is 15,900,000. Grover Cleveland is born in Caldwell, New Jersey.

1840—William Henry Harrison is elected president.

1841—President Harrison dies in Washington, D.C., one month after inauguration. Vice-President John Tyler succeeds him.

1843—William McKinley is born in Niles, Ohio.

1844—James Knox Polk is elected president. Samuel Morse sends first telegraphic message.

1845—Texas and Florida become states. Potato famine in Ireland causes massive emigration from Ireland to U.S. Andrew Jackson dies near Nashville, Tennessee.

1846—Iowa enters the Union. War with Mexico begins.

1847—U.S. captures Mexico City.

1848—Zachary Taylor becomes president. Treaty of Guadalupe Hidalgo ends Mexico-U.S. war. Wisconsin becomes a state.

1849—James Polk dies in Nashville, Tennessee.

1850—President Taylor dies in Washington, D.C.; Vice-President Millard Fillmore succeeds him. California enters the Union, breaking tie between slave and free states.

1852—Franklin Pierce is elected president.

1853—Gadsden Purchase transfers Mexican territory to U.S.

1854—"War for Bleeding Kansas" is fought between slave and free states.

1855—Czar Nicholas I of Russia dies, succeeded by Alexander II.

1856—James Buchanan is elected president. In Massacre of Potawatomi Creek, Kansas-slavers are murdered by free-staters. Woodrow Wilson is born in Staunton, Pennsylvania.

1857—William Howard Taft is born in Cincinnati, Ohio.

1858—Minnesota enters the Union. Theodore Roosevelt is born in New York City.

1859—Oregon becomes a state.

1860—Abraham Lincoln is elected president; South Carolina secedes from the Union in protest.

1861—Arkansas, Tennessee, North Carolina, and Virginia secede. Kansas enters the Union as a free state. Civil War begins.

1862—Union forces capture Fort Henry, Roanoke Island, Fort Donelson, Jacksonville, and New Orleans; Union armies are defeated at the battles of Bull Run and Fredericksburg. Martin Van Buren dies in Kinderhook, New York. John Tyler dies near Charles City, Virginia.

1863—Lincoln issues Emancipation Proclamation: all slaves held in rebelling territories are declared free. West Virginia becomes a state.

1864—Abraham Lincoln is reelected. Nevada becomes a state.

1865—Lincoln is assassinated in Washington, D.C., and succeeded by Andrew Johnson. U.S. Civil War ends on May 26. Thirteenth Amendment abolishes slavery. Warren G. Harding is born in Blooming Grove, Ohio.

1867—Nebraska becomes a state. U.S. buys Alaska from Russia for $7,200,000. Reconstruction Acts are passed.

1868—President Johnson is impeached for violating Tenure of Office Act, but is acquitted by Senate. Ulysses S. Grant is elected president. Fourteenth Amendment prohibits voting discrimination. James Buchanan dies in Lancaster, Pennsylvania.

1869—Franklin Pierce dies in Concord, New Hampshire.

1870—Fifteenth Amendment gives blacks the right to vote.

1872—Grant is reelected over Horace Greeley. General Amnesty Act pardons ex-Confederates. Calvin Coolidge is born in Plymouth Notch, Vermont.

1874—Millard Fillmore dies in Buffalo, New York. Herbert Hoover is born in West Branch, Iowa.

1875—Andrew Johnson dies in Carter's Station, Tennessee.

1876—Colorado enters the Union. "Custer's last stand": he and his men are massacred by Sioux Indians at Little Big Horn, Montana.

1877—Rutherford B. Hayes is elected president as all disputed votes are awarded to him.

1880—James A. Garfield is elected president.

1881—President Garfield is assassinated and dies in Elberon, New Jersey. Vice-President Chester A. Arthur succeeds him.

1882—U.S. bans Chinese immigration. Franklin D. Roosevelt is born in Hyde Park, New York.

1884—Grover Cleveland is elected president.

1885—Ulysses S. Grant dies in Mount McGregor, New York.

1886—Statue of Liberty is dedicated. Chester A. Arthur dies in New York City.

1888—Benjamin Harrison is elected president.

1889—North Dakota, South Dakota, Washington, and Montana become states.

1890—Dwight D. Eisenhower is born in Denison, Texas. Idaho and Wyoming become states.

1892—Grover Cleveland is elected president.

1893—Rutherford B. Hayes dies in Fremont, Ohio.

1896—William McKinley is elected president. Utah becomes a state.

1898—U.S. declares war on Spain over Cuba.

1900—McKinley is reelected. Boxer Rebellion against foreigners in China begins.

1901—McKinley is assassinated by anarchist Leon Czolgosz in Buffalo, New York; Theodore Roosevelt becomes president. Benjamin Harrison dies in Indianapolis, Indiana.

1902—U.S. acquires perpetual control over Panama Canal.

1903—Alaskan frontier is settled.

1904—Russian-Japanese War breaks out. Theodore Roosevelt wins presidential election.

1905 — Treaty of Portsmouth signed, ending Russian-Japanese War.

1906 — U.S. troops occupy Cuba.

1907 — President Roosevelt bars all Japanese immigration. Oklahoma enters the Union.

1908 — William Howard Taft becomes president. Grover Cleveland dies in Princeton, New Jersey. Lyndon B. Johnson is born near Stonewall, Texas.

1909 — NAACP is founded under W.E.B. DuBois

1910 — China abolishes slavery.

1911 — Chinese Revolution begins. Ronald Reagan is born in Tampico, Illinois.

1912 — Woodrow Wilson is elected president. Arizona and New Mexico become states.

1913 — Federal income tax is introduced in U.S. through the Sixteenth Amendment. Richard Nixon is born in Yorba Linda, California. Gerald Ford is born in Omaha, Nebraska.

1914 — World War I begins.

1915 — British liner *Lusitania* is sunk by German submarine.

1916 — Wilson is reelected president.

1917 — U.S. breaks diplomatic relations with Germany. Czar Nicholas of Russia abdicates as revolution begins. U.S. declares war on Austria-Hungary. John F. Kennedy is born in Brookline, Massachusetts.

1918 — Wilson proclaims "Fourteen Points" as war aims. On November 11, armistice is signed between Allies and Germany.

1919 — Eighteenth Amendment prohibits sale and manufacture of intoxicating liquors. Wilson presides over first League of Nations; wins Nobel Peace Prize. Theodore Roosevelt dies in Oyster Bay, New York.

1920 — Nineteenth Amendment (women's suffrage) is passed. Warren Harding is elected president.

1921 — Adolf Hitler's stormtroopers begin to terrorize political opponents.

1922 — Irish Free State is established. Soviet states form USSR. Benito Mussolini forms Fascist government in Italy.

1923 — President Harding dies in San Francisco, California; he is succeeded by Vice-President Calvin Coolidge.

1924 — Coolidge is elected president. Woodrow Wilson dies in Washington, D.C. James Carter is born in Plains, Georgia. George Bush is born in Milton, Massachusetts.

1925 — Hitler reorganizes Nazi Party and publishes first volume of *Mein Kampf.*

1926 — Fascist youth organizations founded in Germany and Italy. Republic of Lebanon proclaimed.

1927 — Stalin becomes Soviet dictator. Economic conference in Geneva attended by fifty-two nations.

1928 — Herbert Hoover is elected president. U.S. and many other nations sign Kellogg-Briand pacts to outlaw war.

1929 — Stock prices in New York crash on "Black Thursday"; the Great Depression begins.

1930 — Bank of U.S. and its many branches close (most significant bank failure of the year). William Howard Taft dies in Washington, D.C.

1931 — Emigration from U.S. exceeds immigration for first time as Depression deepens.

1932 — Franklin D. Roosevelt wins presidential election in a Democratic landslide.

1933 — First concentration camps are erected in Germany. U.S. recognizes USSR and resumes trade. Twenty-First Amendment repeals prohibition. Calvin Coolidge dies in Northampton, Massachusetts.

1934 — Severe dust storms hit Plains states. President Roosevelt passes U.S. Social Security Act.

1936 — Roosevelt is reelected. Spanish Civil War begins. Hitler and Mussolini form Rome-Berlin Axis.

1937 — Roosevelt signs Neutrality Act.

1938 — Roosevelt sends appeal to Hitler and Mussolini to settle European problems amicably.

1939 — Germany takes over Czechoslovakia and invades Poland, starting World War II.

1940—Roosevelt is reelected for a third term.

1941—Japan bombs Pearl Harbor, U.S. declares war on Japan. Germany and Italy declare war on U.S.; U.S. then declares war on them.

1942—Allies agree not to make separate peace treaties with the enemies. U.S. government transfers more than 100,000 Nisei (Japanese-Americans) from west coast to inland concentration camps.

1943—Allied bombings of Germany begin.

1944—Roosevelt is reelected for a fourth term. Allied forces invade Normandy on D-Day.

1945—President Franklin D. Roosevelt dies in Warm Springs, Georgia; Vice-President Harry S. Truman succeeds him. Mussolini is killed; Hitler commits suicide. Germany surrenders. U.S. drops atomic bomb on Hiroshima; Japan surrenders: end of World War II.

1946—U.N. General Assembly holds its first session in London. Peace conference of twenty-one nations is held in Paris.

1947—Peace treaties are signed in Paris. "Cold War" is in full swing.

1948—U.S. passes Marshall Plan Act, providing $17 billion in aid for Europe. U.S. recognizes new nation of Israel. India and Pakistan become free of British rule. Truman is elected president.

1949—Republic of Eire is proclaimed in Dublin. Russia blocks land route access from Western Germany to Berlin; airlift begins. U.S., France, and Britain agree to merge their zones of occupation in West Germany. Apartheid program begins in South Africa.

1950—Riots in Johannesburg, South Africa, against apartheid. North Korea invades South Korea. U.N. forces land in South Korea and recapture Seoul.

1951—Twenty-Second Amendment limits president to two terms.

1952—Dwight D. Eisenhower resigns as supreme commander in Europe and is elected president.

1953—Stalin dies; struggle for power in Russia follows. Rosenbergs are executed for espionage.

1954—U.S. and Japan sign mutual defense agreement.

1955—Blacks in Montgomery, Alabama, boycott segregated bus lines.

1956—Eisenhower is reelected president. Soviet troops march into Hungary.

1957—U.S. agrees to withdraw ground forces from Japan. Russia launches first satellite, *Sputnik.*

1958—European Common Market comes into being. Alaska becomes the forty-ninth state. Fidel Castro begins war against Batista government in Cuba.

1959—Hawaii becomes fiftieth state. Castro becomes premier of Cuba. De Gaulle is proclaimed president of the Fifth Republic of France.

1960—Historic debates between Senator John F. Kennedy and Vice-President Richard Nixon are televised. Kennedy is elected president. Brezhnev becomes president of USSR.

1961—Berlin Wall is constructed. Kennedy and Khrushchev confer in Vienna. In Bay of Pigs incident, Cubans trained by CIA attempt to overthrow Castro.

1962—U.S. military council is established in South Vietnam.

1963—Riots and beatings by police and whites mark civil rights demonstrations in Birmingham, Alabama; 30,000 troops are called out, Martin Luther King, Jr., is arrested. Freedom marchers descend on Washington, D.C., to demonstrate. President Kennedy is assassinated in Dallas, Texas; Vice-President Lyndon B. Johnson is sworn in as president.

1964—U.S. aircraft bomb North Vietnam. Johnson is elected president. Herbert Hoover dies in New York City.

1965—U.S. combat troops arrive in South Vietnam.

1966—Thousands protest U.S. policy in Vietnam. National Guard quells race riots in Chicago.

1967—Six-Day War between Israel and Arab nations.

1968—Martin Luther King, Jr., is assassinated in Memphis, Tennessee. Senator Robert Kennedy is assassinated in Los Angeles. Riots and police brutality take place at Democratic National Convention in Chicago. Richard Nixon is elected president. Czechoslovakia is invaded by Soviet troops.

1969 — Dwight D. Eisenhower dies in Washington, D.C. Hundreds of thousands of people in several U.S. cities demonstrate against Vietnam War.

1970 — Four Vietnam War protesters are killed by National Guardsmen at Kent State University in Ohio.

1971 — Twenty-Sixth Amendment allows eighteen-year-olds to vote.

1972 — Nixon visits Communist China; is reelected president in near-record landslide. Watergate affair begins when five men are arrested in the Watergate hotel complex in Washington, D.C. Nixon announces resignations of aides Haldeman, Ehrlichman, and Dean and Attorney General Kleindienst as a result of Watergate-related charges. Harry S. Truman dies in Kansas City, Missouri.

1973 — Vice-President Spiro Agnew resigns; Gerald Ford is named vice-president. Vietnam peace treaty is formally approved after nineteen months of negotiations. Lyndon B. Johnson dies in San Antonio, Texas.

1974 — As a result of Watergate cover-up, impeachment is considered; Nixon resigns and Ford becomes president. Ford pardons Nixon and grants limited amnesty to Vietnam War draft evaders and military deserters.

1975 — U.S. civilians are evacuated from Saigon, South Vietnam, as Communist forces complete takeover of South Vietnam.

1976 — U.S. celebrates its Bicentennial. James Earl Carter becomes president.

1977 — Carter pardons most Vietnam draft evaders, numbering some 10,000.

1980 — Ronald Reagan is elected president.

1981 — President Reagan is shot in the chest in assassination attempt. Sandra Day O'Connor is appointed first woman justice of the Supreme Court.

1983 — U.S. troops invade island of Grenada.

1984 — Reagan is reelected president. Democratic candidate Walter Mondale's running mate, Geraldine Ferraro, is the first woman selected for vice-president by a major U.S. political party.

1985 — Soviet Communist Party secretary Konstantin Chernenko dies; Mikhail Gorbachev succeeds him. U.S. and Soviet officials discuss arms control in Geneva. Reagan and Gorbachev hold summit conference in Geneva. Racial tensions accelerate in South Africa.

1986 — Space shuttle *Challenger* explodes shortly after takeoff; crew of seven dies. U.S. bombs bases in Libya. Corazon Aquino defeats Ferdinand Marcos in Philippine presidential election.

1987 — Iraqi missile rips the U.S. frigate *Stark* in the Persian Gulf, killing thirty-seven American sailors. Congress holds hearings to investigate sale of U.S. arms to Iran to finance Nicaraguan *contra* movement.

1988 — George Bush is elected president. President Reagan and Soviet leader Gorbachev sign INF treaty, eliminating intermediate nuclear forces. Severe drought sweeps the United States.

Index

Page numbers in boldface type indicate illustrations.

About the Author

Charnan Simon grew up reading anything she could get her hands on in Ohio, Georgia, Oregon, and Washington. She has a B.A. in English Literature from Carleton College in Northfield, Minnesota, and an M.A. in English Literature from the University of Chicago. She worked in children's trade books after college, and then went on to become the managing editor of *Cricket* magazine before beginning her career as a freelance writer. Ms. Simon has written dozens of books and articles for young people and especially likes writing—and reading—history, biography, and fiction of all sorts. She lives in Chicago with her husband and two daughters.